What Should I Do With My Life?

A Guide to Helping You Merge Your Skills, Interests, and Values to Develop and Pursue a Life Purpose

by Aiden Bruneteau

Table of Contents

Introduction 1

Chapter 1: How to Merge Talent with Passion 7

Chapter 2: Anticipating Change 13

Chapter 3: Avoid Sign Hunting 17

Chapter 4: Practice Active Searching 21

Chapter 5: Recognizing Fear as an Obstacle 29

Conclusions 33

Introduction

What should I do with my life? It's a question that will come up during the course of your lifetime, and probably multiple times. It's also a difficult question to answer for a few reasons.

First, it requires you to assess your self-esteem and take a risk. How big do you dare to dream? Are you seeking out a simple life of comfort, enjoying and being grateful for the smallest of things? Are you the type of person who is filled with joy and contentment in the face of rich natural beauty? Or are you captivated by humanity's most luxurious creations, unwilling to let your life pass you by without taking your shot at "the good life." Answering these big questions will help you make some determinations about where you want to live, what industry you want to work in, with whom you wish to associate, and who and when you wish to marry, or whether you wish to marry at all.

Often, when discerning your life's purpose, you'll find a lot of competing interests. At some point, you must trust that no decision you make is going to be a perfect one and that surprise twists and turns will always be around every corner. If you're a spiritual person, faith in God or a higher universal order may alleviate some of the stress of the uncertainty or "not knowing."

This book was written to give you some guidance along your journey. Here you'll find a step-by-step regimen to help you explore your vision for your own life, and take action accordingly. Ready to get started?

Chapter 1: How to Merge Talent with Passion

It would be nice if life were so simple that everyone genuinely enjoyed doing whatever it was they were best at. Unfortunately, this is not reality. All people, whether they're famous musicians, actors, CEOs, astronauts, or waitresses, are forced to face the reality of *work*. For the purpose of this book *work* refers to the obligation to perform some duty that the individual does not always want to perform, but does so anyway in the interest of service and survival.

Consider for example the candid complaints of multi-millionaire radio personality, Howard Stern, who's been known to express on his program the difficulties of getting up every morning for 30+ years before the crack of dawn to prepare for his morning radio show. Sure, he's doing what he'd always dreamed of doing ever since he was a small child, but he's still doing work.

Sure some jobs are cushy, some jobs pay astronomical sums, and other jobs are extremely difficult and pay very little, but regardless of what station you're at in life, work is reality. Aligning with your life purpose doesn't mean that you're free from any obligation or stress, and there's little validity in the quote "Do what you love and you never have to work a day in your life."

Finding fulfillment in life is about finding out what you *should be* doing, not necessarily what you *want to* be dong. That said, knowing what you *want* to do with your life is a key component to knowing what you *should* be doing with your life.

Stop reading this book here and take an hour to think about what you really *want* to do with your life, without focusing so much on monetary gain. Grab a notepad and go for a walk or sit quietly in your room. Take a few deep breaths to slow your mind and write down your thoughts. They can pertain to your personal life or your professional life. They can relate to where you want to live, where you'd like to travel, the types of people you want to meet. Write everything down and see what you come up with after an hour. Don't worry about writing neatly, or in complete sentences. Even half-baked thoughts jotted down are fine.

Are you back? Great. Now for the second part of this exercise, take another hour and write down everything that you're good at. Be sure to include not just skills and talents, but also make a note of the type of people you're best at interacting with. In which social and professional environments do you thrive? Be sure to include those environments or skills in which you thrive but do not necessarily enjoy or feel comfortable. For example, at some level, everyone hates office politics, especially when they're left disadvantaged by them in some way. Yet some of these same people, despite their personal distastes, do well in highly politicized environments.

Or maybe you don't particularly enjoy being the smartest person in the room, but for some reason, you do better in an environment where people are inclined to come to you for help. Take your hour and compile your list of what, with whom, and where you're at your best.

The third part of this exercise is similar to the first two parts. Take another hour and think about the ways in which your unique skill set, temperament or interests could help you *serve others*. You can think of service as something that would benefit others in a charitable way — providing clean water for third world populations, or providing affordable meals for the homeless — or you can think in more economic terms: *"What can I do or produce that other people would be willing to pay me for?"* Take an hour to reflect and write down your findings.

When you have all three of these lists, begin with the first list — things you *want* to do with your life, and score them on a 1 to 10 scale, with 10 next to things you feel are most important and 1 next to things that aren't very important. After you've finished assigning a number to every item on your list, **put a star next to every item that you scored 8 or higher**.

Now, on your second list — things you're good at — score the list on a scale of 1 to 5 based off of the **following criteria:**

1) For skills or aptitudes that don't at all align with any of the items **you have starred** on your first list

2) For skills or aptitudes that barely align with the items **you have starred** on your fist list

9

3) For skills or aptitudes that somewhat align with the items **you have starred** on your fist list

4) For skills or aptitudes that closely align with the items **you have starred** on your first list.

5) For skills or aptitudes that all but exactly align with the items **you have starred** on your first list.

For your third list, create a scoring system similar to the one you used for the second list and see how much overlap you get between what you're passionate about and what you're good at and what you can provide for the world. Look at the skills and aptitudes (list 2) that you've scored at 5. Have you ever considered taking actions that would help you further perfect these abilities? Maybe you should.

If you have little or no alignment between what you really want to do and what you're good at, then your life-purpose discernment process is going to be a little more difficult. It's time to ask yourself whether or not you want to live life in service to others, the planet, God, or whether you want to live life in service to the self. Perhaps it's not fair to involve God in the discussion, perhaps for believers, it was God who put the desire in your heart for whatever it is you truly desire. But if you are reading this book, then you probably don't really have such a clear and commanding sense of purpose. You are probably trying to decipher your purpose amidst a variety of competing values, which is exactly what this book will help you do.

Now, if you're having trouble matching up your list items, and you're a person who's really passionate about giving back to others, try lowering your cut off number a bit; go back to your first list and place a heart (♥) next to every item that scored 5 or higher. See if you can now connect a few more of your aptitudes (list 2) and service opportunities (list 3) with the things you really *want to do* (list 1).

Hold onto these lists and repeat this exercise from scratch after a day, then again after a week, and again after a month. Look to see what's changed and what's stayed the same. Pay close attention to yourself as you generate these lists, the thought processes you follow, your reasoning etc. Are you being influenced by the expectations of your peers? Your family? And if so, are you ok with that? Is it worth it to you to please your family even at the expense of following a path you may not personally be ecstatic about following?

One thing to keep in mind — one of the most common regrets people have when they're close to death is living their lives for the sake of others rather than for themselves. But then almost equally as common are the laments of people who feel that their lives didn't matter enough, that they didn't contribute or give back or love enough. The extent to which you want to live in service to self, family, community, country can't be measured for you. You will have to assess these values on your own. But once you have a good idea of where your fundamental inspiration is coming from, then the exercises in this chapter won't fail to steer you forward on your way!

Chapter 2: Anticipating Change

All too often in life, we begin something so very enthusiastically, whether it's a new job, a new home, pet, relationship. We're so thrilled to be where we are that we don't consider the inevitable lag and satiation that slowly chips away at the novelty of any fortuitous circumstance. When you're choosing what you want to do with your life, you must accept and prepare yourself for the inevitable changes you're bound to experience. If you decide that you want to design video games for a living, brace yourself, because the video games you end up working on in ten years may look nothing like the games you enjoy now.

Before jumping into any endeavor, you'd do well to study its history a bit. Continuing with the video game designer example, have the salaries for game designers been sufficient and consistent over the years? Has the market changed its tastes for game styles and aesthetics? Do you get excited about what's on the horizon in this industry? Would you like to be part of bringing new ideas to life?

Another important thing to consider is how you might change as an individual. Are you always going to want the same things? Are you always going to be interested in the same things? Are you the type of person who changes his mind frequently, who has a hard time sticking with one or another hobby but is constantly jumping to something new?

You also need to ask yourself how your personal pursuits will interrelate with, complement, or threaten your career pursuits. For example, if you're really interested in being a stand-up comedian, but also want a family. You'll have to consider the demands of a job (stand-up comedy) that may not pay very much and keep you on the road most days out of the year, with the demands of being a father, husband, provider etc. If you feel duty-bound to pursue a career in military service, are you comfortable leaving the care of your wife and family to the government should anything happen to you?

Again, life pursuits can vary tremendously and the possible outcomes are likewise limitless. Perhaps being a stand-up comedian and a family man may be more challenging than being a car salesman and a family man, but, as many people will tell you, you have to follow your heart. And if you truly believe in your calling, then your way will be shown to you.

Chapter 3: Avoid Sign Hunting

There once was a boy whose parents were divorced, and he couldn't decide whether he wanted to live with his mother or his father. Well, he did in fact prefer living with his mother in Idaho, because that's where all his friends were. His father was moving to New Jersey for work and he didn't know anyone in New Jersey. Nonetheless, the boy was so afraid that he might hurt his father's feelings, he told himself that he would sit down and work through a Sodoku puzzle. He agreed (with himself) that if he finished the Sodoku puzzle within 5 minutes time that he would give in to his father's wishes and agree to live with him in New Jersey.

He finished the puzzle in 4 minutes and 48 seconds. Afterwards he called his father and told him the news. He was going to move to New Jersey. Six months later, he missed his mother and his friends so badly that he ended up running away from his father's house and returning to Idaho to live with his mom. Throughout the entire process, everyone suffered, and it could have all been avoided if the boy had just listened to his own best judgment and gut instincts.

Here we have an example of a child overwhelmed by fear and uncertainty, desperately attempting to place the onus of his decision on some entity outside himself.

We as humans love to be directed during difficult times. It takes away some of the responsibility and murkiness of a difficult decision if we feel that we are being directed by God or the universe in some particular direction. Deciding what to do with your life is often an extremely difficult decision. And we are thus tempted to look for external signals, signs, or advice, something to grab onto outside of ourselves, like the passing advice of a friend, the pressures of a parent, or the random result of a Sodoku puzzle.

As adults, we must not sacrifice our rational faculty when making big decisions about the directions of our lives. For decisions of such high importance it's all the more crucial that we apply the utmost in sound and rational judgment. Many people get intimidated by this prospect because they know that a question so vast cannot be answered perfectly. We don't have the luxury of dictating every element of our life journey. But we are able to control and discern some things, and we're certainly able to control more of our destiny than anyone else can control. If the little boy from our story had had the courage to listen to his own difficult, yet best available, evaluation of his circumstance, he could have saved his family and himself from much tumult, stress, and worry.

The first thing to remember when making big, important, and difficult decisions about your life is that you're going to have to take action based on limited information. The trick to doing this with maximum comfort and confidence is to acknowledge when you've done all you could do to evaluate whatever decision it is you need to make. From that point forward you may be proceeding with limited and imperfect information, but you still have every right to proceed with confidence and a hopeful spirit.

Imagine life as a vast cave and all you have to guide you is a small, still, but persistent candle. Even though that candle can only light small portions of the cave at any given time, it is still the most important navigational tool you have at-hand. Also, standing still in the cave with the candle will get you nowhere, so you much make a choice and move forward in one direction to have any hope of finding your way.

Chapter 4: Practice Active Searching

So you've assessed your passions and the extent to which they line up with your talents. You've assessed your values and determined what's most important to you in life. And you're still having trouble.

Fear not! When it comes to uncovering purpose in your life, getting there is half the fun. You're not going to learn more about yourself just by being idle. If you want to find out what you want out of life, then you need to be proactive. Here are some pursuits that will help expedite your journey to a life of direction and fulfillment:

Go Back To School

Even if you're not sure what it is you want to study, go take some adult education courses on a whim. You'll expose yourself to not only new knowledge and skills, but also to new people. Engaging academic settings often force you to think creatively and be introspective.

Try New Things, Especially Those Outside of Your Comfort Zone

If you've never been kayaking, rock climbing, or skiing; if you've never sung in a chorus or took oboe lessons; if you've never joined a community theater, or volunteered at a homeless shelter; now's the time! Doing new things allows you to meet new people, experience new environments, and touch new depths in your own personal character. You may have been sitting on an uncanny treasure of natural jiu jitsu skills, but for shame, you never knew because you'd never taken a jiu jitsu lesson. Maybe you've got the voice of the next American pop icon, but because you've never been taught by a trained musician, you were none the wiser for it.

It can be especially useful to try things that fall outside of your general comfort zone. There's a peculiar burst of energy we get from staring down and vanquishing our fears. Often moments of clarity, lucidity, and compete freedom ensue. We learn that we're actually capable of lot more than we thought.

Analyze Your Role Models

Is there anyone you know, personally or otherwise, whom you wish you could be like? Take a few moments and think about this person. Do you feel they have a clear understanding of their purpose in life? How do you think they were able to discern that purpose? If you can, research or interview one of your role models. Trace their life trajectory. Did they always know that they were meant to be doing what they ended up doing? Did they begin doing something else? Were they ever unsure or anxious about their career? Are they still unsure or anxious? What were the key events or realizations that led to their development of a strong sense of purpose? Hopefully, doing these role model analyses will help you realize that everyone is lost from time to time, and it's ok to not know exactly what you want to do.

Some very interesting and accomplished people didn't really make their mark on the world until late in life. Hard work and confidence can lubricate the gears, but ultimately inspiration is its own machine and it operates according to its own time line.

Find a Life Coach

They're everywhere. Life coaching is a profession that's taken the world by storm. A life coach is a mix of a counsellor and a motivational therapist. Life coaches often have certain specialties and you should choose your life coach accordingly. If you are thinking about starting your own business, then a business life coach would be a good fit for you. If you are a person who values health and wellness, then a wellness life coach might be a good choice, or perhaps even a personal trainer.

Think of the immense value of having someone in your corner whose explicit purpose is to help drive you forward towards your purpose. Even if you're unsure about what that purpose is, a good life coach will provide a constructive dialog you can use to assist your search.

Keep an Attitude Journal

If a new activity, hobby, or profession is something that you may want to continue with on a permanent basis, then you should be able to feel it at a deep level. For example, if you decide to work as a teacher's aide at a high school and you find yourself becoming happy when you go to work and you look forward to being at work, then you may be cut out to be teacher. Something creeps into us when we find something to do that we really love doing. We begin to feel that whatever we are doing is something we could do for the rest of our lives.

If you think you might be experiencing this type of feeling, whether it's happening in a McDonald's or in the US Senate, take note of it. Literally even, start keeping a journal of how you feel while going into work. How often is that feeling present where you feel like you're exactly where you're supposed to be? You're of course going to have days in any job — dream jobs included — where you just don't want to be at work. But if you find that you're in a really comfortable head and heart space for the majority of the time you spend at a given job or activity, then you're probably on to something worth paying attention to.

Meditate

One way to let your purpose manifest is to let your mind air out a bit. Meditation can help you stabilize your thoughts and push through the many distractions of life that can get in the way of your finding your destined purpose.

You have many options when it comes to meditation formats and schools. Among them — Shambhala, Transcendental,

Vipassana. There is no start-up expense for this hobby. All you need is you. In fact, here's a great Vipassana Mindfulness book by Chaya Rao on Amazon:

www.amazon.com/dp/B00NQHE0N2/

Get Connected

One of the best ways to learn if a certain hobby or profession is right for you is to engage others who have devoted significant time and energy pursuing said hobby or profession.

The internet and social media make it easy to engage communities that center around your interests. Funny as it sounds though, engaging these communities and actually developing your online social and professional networks takes time and a degree of discipline. A good solution is to set aside a certain window of time daily or weekly to engage online communities that are relevant to you.

Experience a "Say Yes to Everything Day"

This is something really fun that you can do with a friend on a day when both of you have lots of time to spare. Go out to a coffee shop and find their bulletin board. Find the first flyer that attracts your attention and whatever it's inviting you to do or see, say yes. Go to a speed dating night. Go see a random punk band play in a dive bar. Participate in a research study at the local university. Donate sperm. Just say yes and add the event to your calendar. Continue upholding your "yes to everything" disposition for the rest of the day. If a friend invites you to a party that sounds lame, go. If a man on the street asks you for change, give him some change (then run away before he can ask you for more!). If a palm reader asks you if you'd like your fortune told, do it! You'll end up having a lot of fun and you'll probably end up learning something about yourself.

Nothing's More Powerful than Positivity

Perhaps your most important asset in your search for your life's meaning is a positive attitude. Try to find and appreciate all the good things about your current life station, no matter how murky the future might seem.

Chapter 5: Recognizing Fear as an Obstacle

There was once a man who was vacationing in the summer on the beach in Destin, Florida. The weather was spectacular! The sands were white and the ocean was clean and blue. There was only one drawback: Jellyfish. It was a time of year when Destin's jellyfish population surged along the coastal waters. If you went knee deep into the ocean, you could see them, here and there, spaced out in radii of twenty feet or so. They weren't saturating the water, but they were prevalent enough to make any sea swimmer take pause.

The man had never been stung by a jelly fish before and had no idea how much or how little the sting would hurt. Not knowing what he was potentially in for made him very wary while swimming in the ocean and he had a hard time relaxing. He was constantly on the lookout for jellyfish.

The man eventually realized that he was not making the most of his vacation time, and decided to put an end to his ignorance. He reached out and pressed his palm against the next jellyfish he saw and took measure of the sting. It was unpleasant but not as shrill as he'd feared. Certainly not worth being too cautious about. From that point forward, the man was able to relax and enjoy his time swimming in the ocean.

The jellyfish story not only illustrates how confronting our fears can expand our freedoms, but it also illustrates how our fears can work as obstacles to prevent us from discovering what we are meant to do and who we are meant to be.

How sadly common is the story of the person who really wants to do something or be someone, but doesn't believe in herself. Her negative thoughts hold her back from realizing her goals. Fear of failure is what prevents us at times from trying our best at something. Furthermore, we're afraid that we will look especially silly if we try really hard and still fail. So it's often our choice to simply not try and therefore we sell ourselves short.

The best way to remedy this fear is to learn to accept, even embrace failure. Every great success story has failure (usually a succession of failures) as its backdrop. There's no way to bypass failure if you're end goal is to be successful. Once we learn to see failure as something to be worn like a badge of honor, then we're free to continue shamelessly swinging for the fences until something gets knocked clear out of the park.

Conclusions

Regardless of how old you are or how many fits and starts you've already pushed through in your life, you still may be at a place where you're not sure how to best use your talents and skills towards your utmost personal fulfillment.

Anyone who finds himself in this predicament should at very least undertake the exercise described in the first chapter of this book. The "Active Searching" activities described in chapter 4 may be a bit much to take on all at once. Choose two activities from the list to pursue immediately, and integrate the others as needed.

Don't expect a sense of direction and personal fulfillment to transform you overnight. Though there are eureka moments in life, discovering your direction is always a work in progress. Even after you've got the job you know you're supposed to have, even after you've got your dream house, family, friends, your life will still find ways to hurl questions at you that won't be able to answer right away. Be forever patient with yourself and keep a bright positive attitude, remembering that it's the journey that really counts.

Finally, I'd like to thank you for purchasing this book! If you enjoyed it or found it helpful, I'd greatly appreciate it if you'd take a moment to leave a review on Amazon. Thank you!

Made in the USA
San Bernardino, CA
26 November 2018